Silk Ribbon Flowers

Ann Cox

First published in 2015

Search Press Limited
Wellwood, North Farm Road,
Tunbridge Wells, Kent TN2 3DR

Photographs by Paul Bricknell at
Search Press Studios

Print ISBN: 978-1-78221-107-5
EPUB ISBN: 978-1-78126-238-2

Suppliers
If you have difficulty in obtaining any of the materials and equipment mentioned in this book, then please visit the Search Press website for details of suppliers: www.searchpress.com

Printed in China

Dedication

Ashley, thank you for everything.

Acknowledgements

Another big thank you to Search Press and in particular my editor, May Corfield, for her expertise and enthusiasm throughout. Also to Juan and Paul for their styling and photography respectively on this book – all part of the super team that makes Search Press.

Publisher's Note

You are invited to visit the author's website:
www.anncoxsilkribbons.co.uk

Contents

Introduction

Flowers touch our lives every single day: cherry blossom, wild flowers in a meadow, a perfect rose or delicate spring flowers are a promise of things to come, wherever we may live. As artists and designers, the beauty of all this is that we can recreate what we see or use it as inspiration for our own imaginary flowers.

Silk ribbon is so fine it can be threaded into a needle and embroidered using a few basic embroidery stitches. Each stitch will make a petal or part petal, making it quick to create flowers such as fuchsias, peonies, roses and rosebuds, daisies and many more. It is perfect for embroidering directly on to children's clothes, belts, bags, hairbands and cushions, or to decorate a hair slide or pin to embellish a jacket.

Once you have worked a few flowers, don't be afraid to experiment. Using either a wider or narrower ribbon will alter the size of a flower; removing or adding petals will alter the shape. You don't have to replicate nature – flower shapes and colours are limitless, so let your imagination run riot. Just remember to have fun and enjoy what you do.

Silk ribbon is a friendly medium to work with and you do not need any special skills, but it is important to learn how to control the ribbon to its maximum effect. Please take a few minutes to read through the techniques and tips on pages 6, 7 and 48, and refer to the stitch diagrams on these pages as you work. These show the basic techniques used to control the ribbon to create three-dimensional petals and leaves – quick to do and very effective. Happy sewing!

Know-how and techniques

Choice of fabric You can embroider on any fabric that allows a needle to pass through and does not fray easily. I have used a linen-cotton mix fabric. A piece of fabric that is too small to go into a hoop can be stitched as a patch on to a piece of scrap fabric, which can then be cut away behind the area to be embroidered.

Needles Chenille needles, which have a sharp point and a large eye, are used for silk ribbon embroidery. It is essential to make the right size hole for the ribbon to pass through, but which still allows the ribbon to be controlled. A size 24 chenille needle is used for 2mm ribbon, size 18 for 4mm and 7mm ribbon, and the very large size 13 for 13mm ribbon. A size 8 embroidery needle is used for embroidery threads.

Threads A selection of stranded embroidery threads, and other types of threads for texture are useful, as are pieces of string. Use an embroidery thread that tones with your fabric to anchor ribbon.

Other items used

For each project in this book, you will need a pair of **small, sharp scissors** to cut the ribbon and some **paper scissors** for the templates; for most projects you will also need an **embroidery hoop** to keep the fabric taut and smooth. A **fine, sharp pencil**, **ruler** or **tape measure** and **dressmaking pins** will also be needed.

Cutting and anchoring ribbon

Always cut ribbon at an angle of 45° to prevent fraying, and use a short length – 30cm (12in) is ideal. To begin, 2mm and 4mm ribbon is knotted at one end. For the wider 7mm and 13mm ribbon, a short end (tag end) is threaded into a size 18 or 13 needle and pulled sharply through to the back of the fabric, then secured with a few small stitches behind the petal about to be worked using a fabric-toned embroidery thread. The ribbon needs to sit smoothly on the right side of the fabric. When anchoring ribbon, place the eye end of a second needle between the ribbon and the fabric on the front; this gives enough space to work a few small stitches to secure the ribbon, but not go through the ribbon on the front.

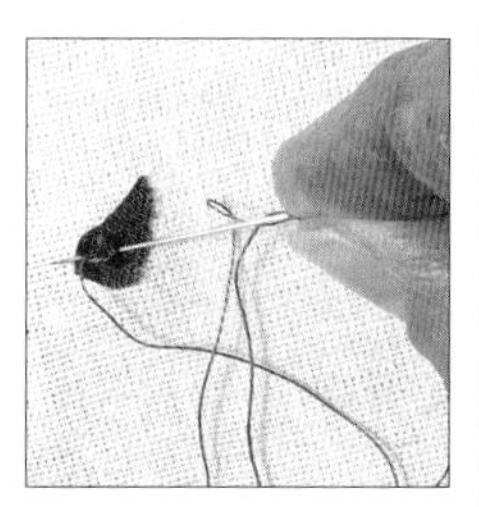

Transferring a design

Trace or photocopy the template on to a piece of paper, cut it out and pin on the fabric with two or more pins; place in an embroidery frame if used. Following project instructions, use a large needle to make a hole through the paper and fabric, then use a fine, sharp pencil to make a dot through the holes to mark the fabric. Remove the template. Never draw in lines or shapes unless individual instructions ask you to do so.

Controlling the ribbon

A second needle the same size as the one used for the ribbon is used to control ribbon on the right side of your work and shape petals for most silk ribbon embroidery. Where the ribbon comes up through the fabric on the front, place the eye end of a second needle under the ribbon to smooth or untwist it, and place a finger on the needle to keep the ribbon smooth and taut as it is pulled through to the back of the fabric (see diagram below).

Short lines like this on a template indicate where to position the eye of your second needle to help shape the petal or leaf tip.

Basic stitches

The simplest stitch used in silk ribbon embroidery is **straight stitch** and is worked by bringing the ribbon up through the fabric and down again, pulling it over the eye of a needle to control the shape (see diagram below).

To make flower stems, you can use embroidery thread and use **couch stitch** (see diagram and photograph below) to curve the stems.

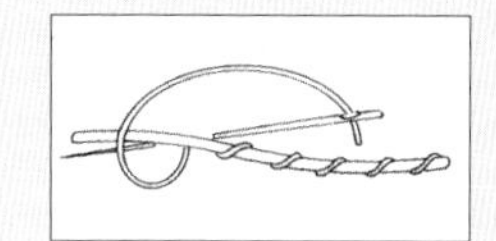

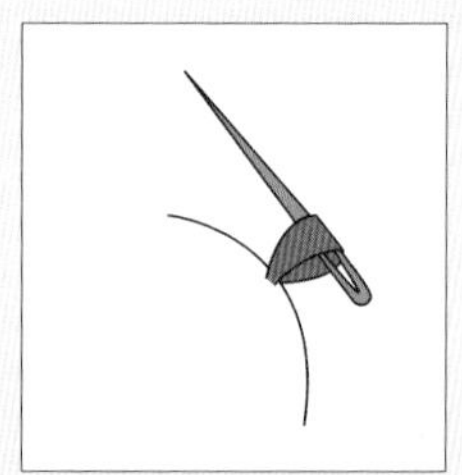

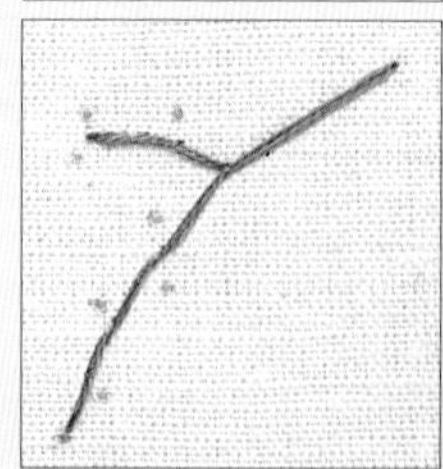

Ribbon stitch is very useful for making different kinds of petals and leaves, and is unique to silk ribbon embroidery.

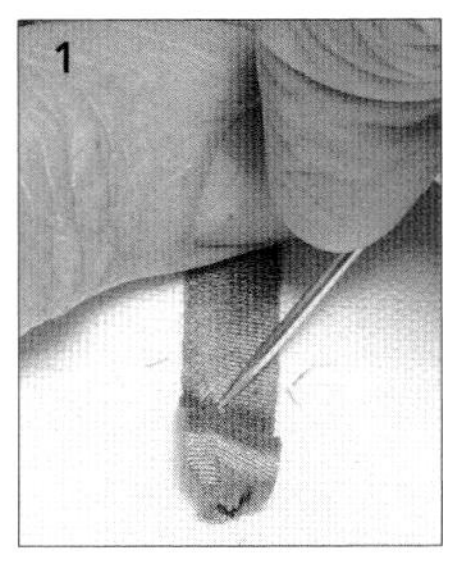

1 Take a short end of the ribbon to the back of the fabric and secure it (see opposite). Thread the ribbon into a needle at the front and form a small loop, then take the needle and ribbon through to the back of the fabric.

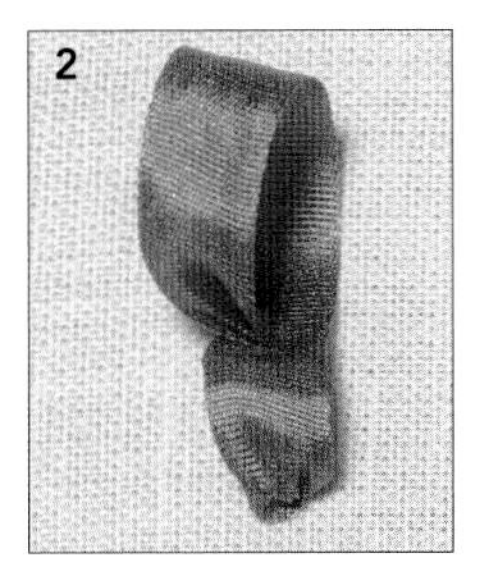

2 Hold the ribbon close to the back of the fabric and gently pull it through a short length at a time.

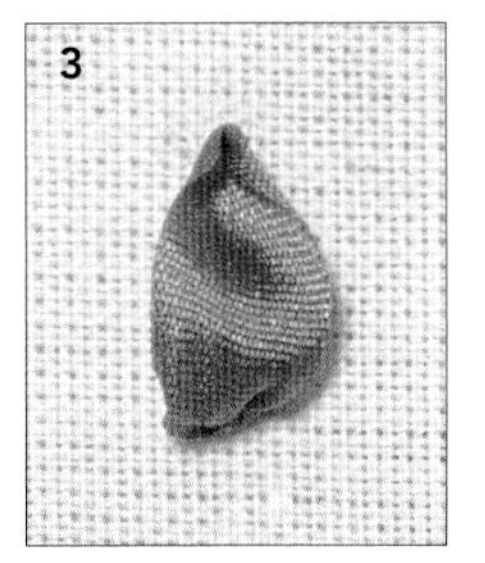

3 Stop pulling as soon as the stitch is formed, when you can see the ribbon just start to curl in on itself and begin to disappear.

French knots are used widely in silk ribbon embroidery.

1 Anchor the ribbon, hold the point of a needle behind the ribbon coming up through the fabric, and wrap it once round the needle. (You can make a 2-loop or 3-loop French knot by wrapping the ribbon round the needle twice or three times.)

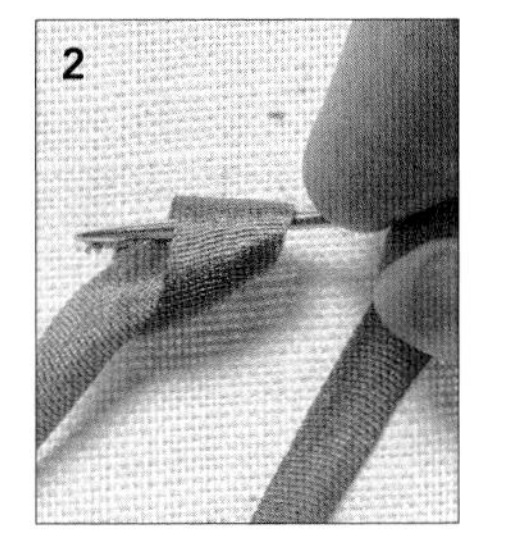

2 Hold the ribbon on the eye of the needle and then push the needle back through the fabric close to where the ribbon comes up.

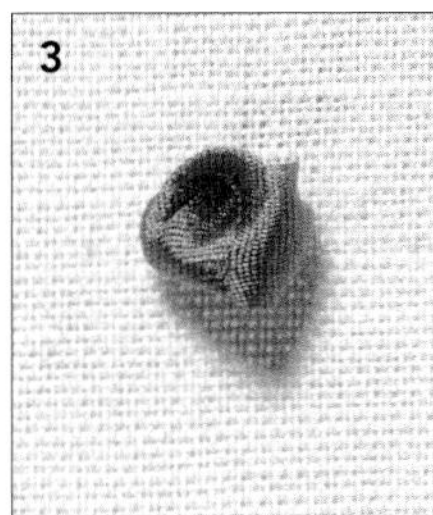

3 Carefully start to pull the ribbon through to the back of the fabric.

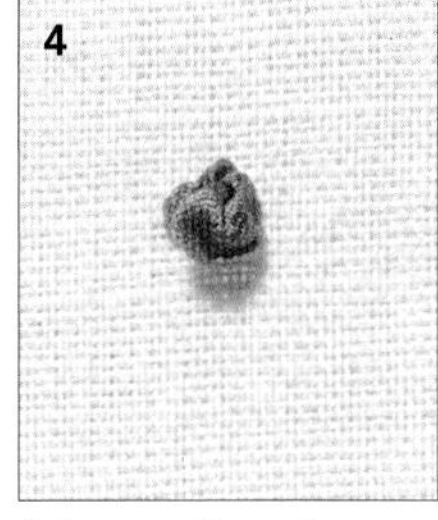

4 Stop pulling when the loop in the riibbon disappears into the knot. This will make a loose knot (see 3). Pull the ribbon tighter to make a smaller knot (see above).

Lazy daisy stitch is worked as follows:

1

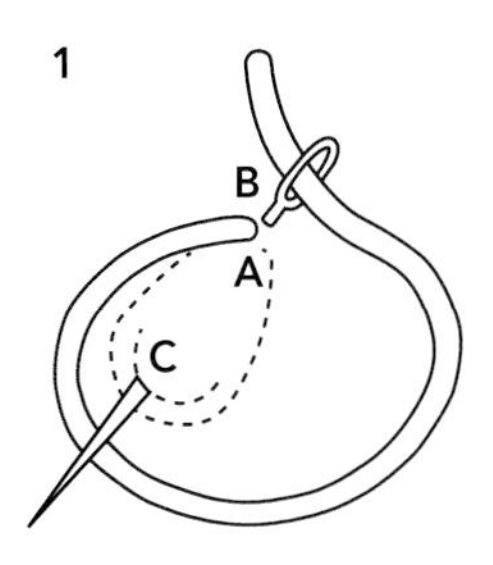

2

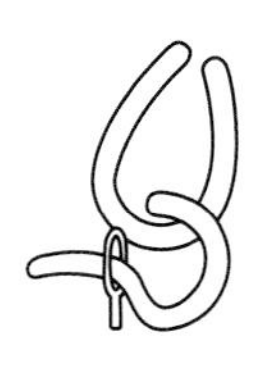

1 Thread a strand of embroidery thread into a needle and knot one end. Bring the needle up through the fabric at A and back down at B, leaving a loop at the front. Now bring the needle up to the front again at C.

2 Gently pull the thread to the desired shape, then take the needle over the loop and back down again at C to complete the stitch.

Peony

Materials:

3m (3¼yd) each of 4mm ribbon in pink and pale pink

1m (39in) of 13mm ribbon in pink

25cms (10in) of 4mm ribbon in deep moss green

Embroidery thread in pale green, pale brown and a fabric tone

Needles:

2 x size 13 needles, 2 x size 18 needles and 1 x size 8 embroidery needle

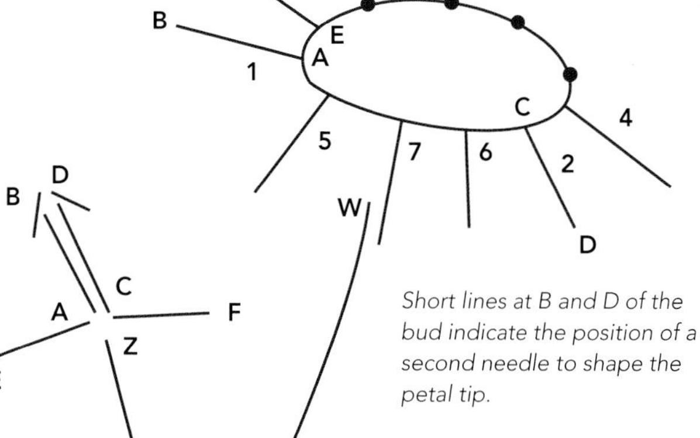

Short lines at B and D of the bud indicate the position of a second needle to shape the petal tip.

Instructions:

1 First, transfer the design on to your fabric. Make a dot at each end of petals 1–7, and along the top of the curved edge. Leave two pins in the lower half of the template, remove the top pins and fold back the top half of the template. Then lightly draw in the oval shape and the lines of the petals, as on the template. Replace the template to mark the position of the bud, calyx and stem (WXYZ), then remove the template. Do not draw in the stem, as these lines will show; only draw in the lines for the petals and calyx of the bud.

2 To make the outer petals, thread a length of 13mm pink ribbon into a size 13 needle, take a short end through the fabric at A of petal 1, and secure with a few small stitches. Rethread the needle with the ribbon on the right side and take it down at B, using the eye end of a second large needle to pull the ribbon over to make a smooth petal with a rounded tip (see Tip 6, page 48). Stop pulling, remove the second needle, secure the ribbon with a few small stitches behind the petal just worked and cut the ribbon at an angle. Secure each petal as it is worked and cut the ribbon, then work petals 2–7 in order, giving slightly more fullness to petals 5, 6 and 7 across the centre.

3 To make the looped centre petals, cut a length of 4mm pale pink ribbon, knot one end and thread it into a size 18 needle. Bring the needle up through between petals 5 and 7 on the drawn line, back down close to where it came up and, using the eye end of a second needle to pull the ribbon over, stop pulling when a 1.5cm ($\frac{5}{8}$in) loop is formed (see diagram on page 10). Taking care not to pull the loop tight, bring the needle up close to the first petal and continue working loops along to petal 4. Alternate the colours each time a new length of ribbon is required until the centre is filled. See Tip 4 (page 48) to prevent stitching through ribbon on the wrong side of the fabric.

4 To make the bud, using 13mm pink ribbon, work a single straight stitch from A to B, placing a second needle as indicated on the template, to shape the tip as the ribbon is pulled over (see Tip 6, page 48). Fasten off. Repeat for petal CD as shown to create the bud. Fasten off.

5 To make the calyx, anchor the end of a length of 4mm deep moss ribbon at A and work ribbon stitch at E, then bring the needle up at C and repeat at F. Fasten off.

6 For the stem, make a stem thread with three strands each of green and brown, thread into a needle and knot one end. Bring the needle up at W, down at X and up at Y, pass the eye of the needle under WX then take it down at Z to kink stem WX. Fasten off. Work couch stitch with a strand of toning thread along stems WX and ZY to give them a slight curve.

Zinnia

Materials:

1.5m (1¾yd) each of 7mm ribbon in cyclamen, deep pink and deep mauve

Embroidery threads in deep red, deep pink, pale green and fabric tone

Needles:

2 x size 18 needles and 1 x size 8 embroidery needle

Instructions:

1 First, draw a design of three circles on some paper, one inside the other (see below): one of 2cm (¾in), one of 3cm (1¼in) and one of 4cm (1½in). To transfer the design, cut round the outer circle, pin it in place on the fabric, then either draw or tack a line round the template (but not through the paper). Keeping the template in place, cut round the middle circle to remove the outer paper ring and repeat for the centre, so you now have three circles marked on the fabric. Remove the centre template.

2 To make the flower centre, use two strands each of deep red and deep pink thread, and one of pale green together, thread them into a size 18 needle and knot one end (see Tip 5, page 48). Bring the needle up in the centre and work a triangle of three 2-loop French knots. Continue working rounds to fill the centre, ending with a final round of 1-loop French knots to complete. Fasten off.

3 To make the petals, thread a size 18 needle with a length of cyclamen ribbon and secure at the edge of the French knots. Now take the needle down 2mm (1/16in) away from where it came up, radiating out from the centre, at the same time as using the eye end of a second needle to pull the ribbon over to make a petal of 1.25cm (½in) (see the diagram below). Stop pulling. Continue working petals round next to each other, so that they always radiate outwards towards the edge of the flower. Fasten off.

4 Work the next round of petals using deep pink ribbon, and the outer ring with deep mauve ribbon to complete the flower. Reverse these colours to make the second flower.

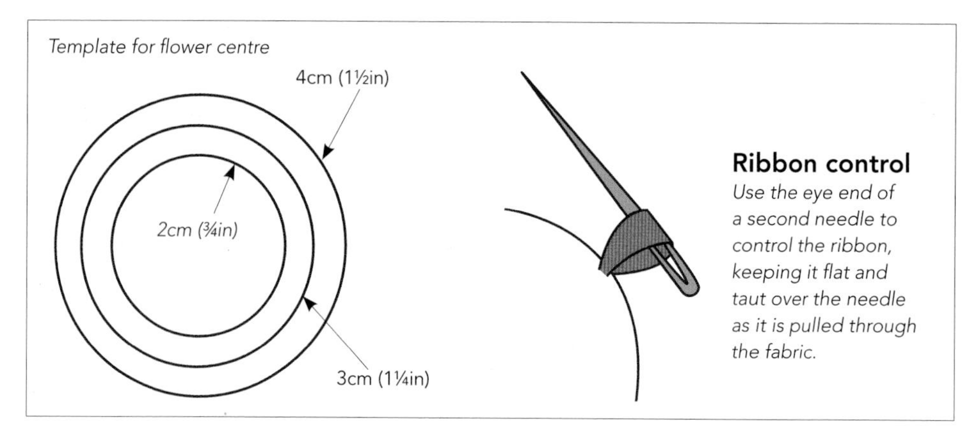

Ribbon control

Use the eye end of a second needle to control the ribbon, keeping it flat and taut over the needle as it is pulled through the fabric.

This flower has been worked in three colours, with the colours reversed for the upper one.

Cornflower

Materials:

3m (3¼yd) each of 4mm ribbon in delphinium blue and violet

Embroidery thread in deep blue, pale blue, white and fabric tone

Optional: blue silky thread of a different tone

Needles:

2 x size 18 needles and 1 x size 8 embroidery needle

Instructions:

1 Use the template (right) to transfer the 1.25cm (½in) diameter flower centre on to the fabric. Then thread one strand of deep blue, two strands of pale blue and one of white embroidery thread into a size 18 needle and knot one end (see Tip 5, page 48). Work a triangle of three 2-loop French knots in the centre, then continue working round to fill the centre. Fasten off.

2 To make the petals, thread a length of ribbon into a size 18 needle and knot one end. Bring the needle up at the edge of the French knots and take it back down, next to where it came up, using the eye end of a second needle to keep the loop taut as it is pulled through to the back. Stop pulling when you have formed a 1.5cm (⅝in) loop. Taking care not to pull the ribbon and shorten the loop, turn the fabric over to the wrong side and work a secure knot, as shown in the diagram (right). Bring the needle up close to the last loop (see Tip 3, page 48), leaving a small gap; repeat the process, knotting each loop as it is worked.

3 Join in the other colour each time a new length of ribbon is required, in order to mix the tones, then work a second round, filling the gaps.

4 When complete, cut through each loop at an angle with a pair of small, sharp scissors to create petals. To add extra texture, I have used a silky thread to work a few short loops at random in the French knot centre, which are then cut.

Template for flower centre: 1.25cm (½in) in diameter

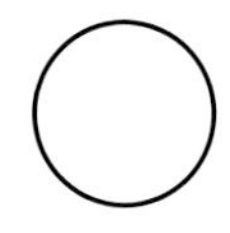

Securing knots for cut loops

This type of knot will prevent petals being pulled out of the fabric when the loops are cut at the end.

Wrap the ribbon round the needle as shown, taking care not to pull the loop at the front of the fabric. Now pull the ribbon firmly round the needle as it is taken through to the front ready for the next petal.

This pretty cornflower makes a perfect embellishment for the strap of a shoulder bag.

Carnation

Materials:

20cm (8in) of 13mm ribbon in pink

33cm (13in) each of 13mm ribbon in pale pink and cream

33cm (13in) of 4mm ribbon in leaf green

Pale blue/green tapestry wool

Toning embroidery threads

Needles:

1 x size 13 needle, 1 x size 18 needle and 1 x size 8 embroidery needle

Instructions:

1 To make the carnation with the stem, cut one end of the mid-pink ribbon at an angle, thread a size 8 embroidery needle with a toning thread and work a tiny stitch over the selvedge to secure the knot, as shown in the diagram on page 42. Work tiny running stitches across the cut end of the ribbon and then along the selvedge until 2.5cm (1in) from the end. Now work back across at an angle – do not cut the thread, but cut the ribbon at an angle 1cm (½in) from the stitch line as shown on page 42. Repeat for the other two ribbons (see page 6 for information on anchoring and controlling ribbon).

2 Place a size 13 needle into the fabric and thread the knotted end of the ribbon into the needle, then sharply pull this end through so that the angled stitch line sits in the thickness of the fabric. Secure with toning thread. Then bring the needle and thread up through the fabric, close to the ribbon. Lightly gather the first 10cm (4in), hold the ribbon out to one side with the gathered edge on the fabric, pass the point of the needle through the ribbon about 1cm (½in) along (just above but not through the gathering stitches) and use it to pull the ribbon round. Take the needle back down, then bring it up again about 5mm (¼in) along.

3 Continue for three to four rounds, then gradually increase the gathering as you work round, always securing tight to the gathered ribbon already secured. To fasten off, take the end of the ribbon and gathering thread through to the back at an angle as before, hold the petals firmly, and gently pull the gathering thread to seat the petals; fasten off securely with this thread. Repeat for the mid-tone but leave sufficient gathered ribbon to fold back just above halfway, to give an extra row round the lower half. Fasten off, then use the cream ribbon, gathered slightly more, and work two half rows as before. Fasten off.

4 To make the calyx, cut out the template below, place in the centre under the flower and lightly draw in the U-shape. Using the wool, work four to five small stitches across as shown for padding, then bring the needle up at A and down at B and so on to fill the shape. Fasten off.

5 To make the stem, work one long straight stitch using the wool, from the calyx to the base of the stem and back up to secure behind the calyx. Couch in place with a toning thread.

6 To make each leaf, work a ribbon stitch from the stem to the tip using green ribbon, fastening off after each pair. Work more leaves, allowing some to twist, as in the photograph.

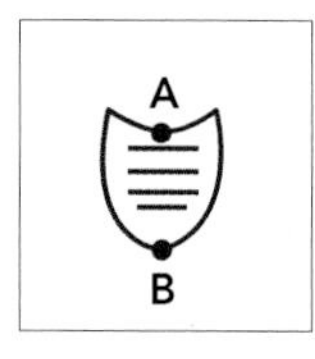

Calyx template

The carnation above is toned from mid- to pale pink with cream outer petals, but any colour or combination of colours could be used. Gathering different lengths of ribbon will create any size flower that you wish.

Fuchsia

Materials:

75cm (30in) of 7mm ribbon in pink for the petals

50cm (20in) of 7mm ribbon in pale pink for the sepals and bud

20cm (8in) of 4mm ribbon in pale pink for the tube

33cm (13in) of 7mm ribbon in green for the leaves

15cm (6in) of 4mm ribbon in green for the ovary

Embroidery threads in pink, green and fabric colour

Needles:

2 x size 18 needles and 1 x size 8 embroidery needle

Instructions:

1 Mark each end of the petals, sepals and leaves on the fabric, then lightly draw in a line for each petal and leaf, but not the sepals, as lines will show. Make a dot for the stigma and each stamen.

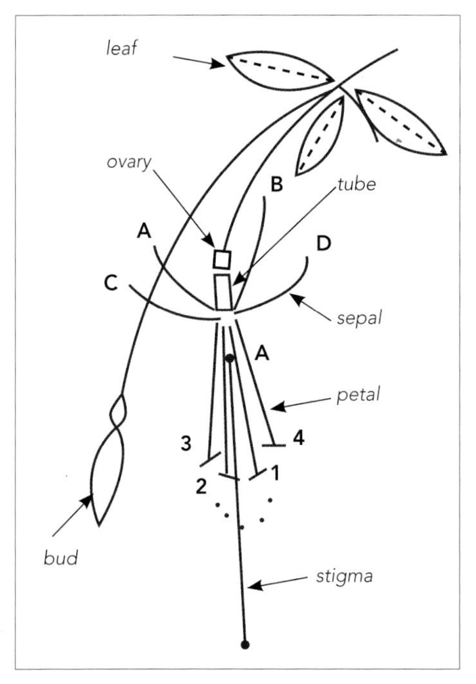

2 Anchor the 7mm pink ribbon at the top of petal 1 and work a straight stitch through at the base, then petal 2 (see Tips 6 and 7, page 48). Work petals 3 and 4, making both slightly fuller. Fasten off. Use 7mm pale pink ribbon to work sepals A and B in ribbon stitch; use straight stitch with a slight lift for C and D. Fasten off. Make the tube above the petals in straight stitch, using 4mm pale pink ribbon, and the ovary in 4mm green ribbon.

3 To make the bud, use 7mm pale pink ribbon and work in straight stitch from the top to the tip. Use two strands of embroidery thread in the same colour to work a few small stitches 3mm (1/8in) from the top of the bud to pull the ribbon in and make a tube, as in the diagram.

4 To make the stigma and stamens, bring the needle up at A each time: use two strands of thread and straight stitch for the stigma with a 1-loop French knot at the end, then use a single strand to repeat for the stamens.

5 To make the stem, use two strands of embroidery thread and work a straight stitch but do not fasten off. To make the stem curve, couch over the thread using a single strand of thread. Fasten off both threads.

6 To make the leaves, work some in ribbon stitch and some in straight stitch, from the stem to the tip at random.

Template flower and bud

Anemone

Materials:

1m (39in) of 7mm ribbon for each flower – I used light mauve, dark red, soft blue, cyclamen, dusky red, delphinium blue, soft poppy red and deep mauve

Black, white and fabric colour embroidery thread

Needles:

2 x size 18 needles, 1 x size 24 needle and 1 x size 8 embroidery needle

Instructions:

1 Transfer the dots of the inner and outer circles on to your fabric and remove the template. Taking care to be accurate, lightly draw a short line from the centre of ribbon stitch (RS) petal 1, as indicated on the template. Repeat for RS petal 2, then 3, 4, 5, and 6. Petals are worked in two rounds; first, the RS petals and second, the straight stitch (SS) petals.

2 Take the end of a length of 7mm ribbon through to the back of the fabric at A of petal RS1 and secure behind the petal to be worked. Flatten the ribbon with this needle, then take it down through the centre of the ribbon at the dot, placing the eye end of a second needle in the loop formed to pull the ribbon over. Keep the needle in place as the ribbon is brought up to the front for the next stitch. Remove the second needle and gently pull the ribbon to shape to complete the ribbon stitch, then work petals 2–6 and fasten off. Now work the SS petals round in order between each of the RS petals, then fasten off.

3 The stamens are made by working French knots. Thread three strands of black embroidery thread into a size 24 needle, knot one end and work a 2-loop French knot in the centre. Work two rounds, then work 1-loop French knots to fill the rest of the flower centre. Fasten off. Using two strands of white embroidery thread, work 1-loop French knots at intervals round between the petals and black French knots. Fasten off to complete.

Template

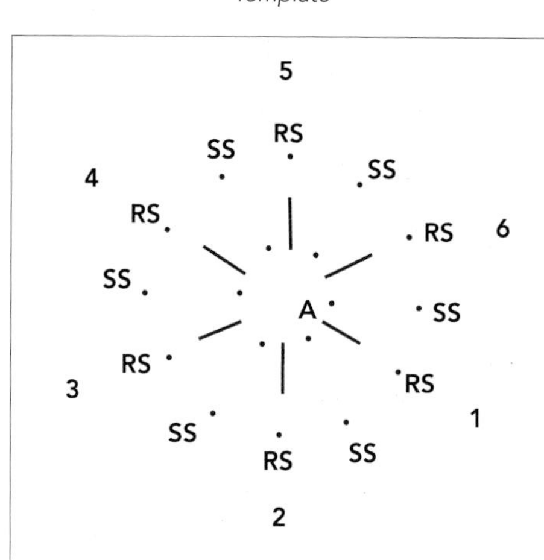

RS = ribbon stitch, SS = straight stitch

Numbers 1–6 indicate RS petals

Lacecap Hydrangea

Materials:

Approx. 120cm (47in) of 7mm ribbon for each flower. Each floret requires approx. 12cm (5in) of 7mm ribbon – I used sky blue, soft blue, dusky rose and rose pink

Embroidery threads to tone, plus pale green, white and fabric colour

Needles:

2 x size 18 needles, 1 x size 24 needle and 1 x size 8 embroidery needle

Instructions:

1 The sizes and shapes of these flowers are deliberately worked at random. To start, cut out a template the size and shape of the flower you wish to work as a guide – there is no need to draw in the florets. Place it on the fabric and tack a line round the outside edge to give a boundary to work within. Refer to the diagram below to draw in a few florets as a guide.

2 To make the florets, secure a length of 7mm ribbon in your chosen colour at the centre of petal 1. Now take the needle down at the tip, using the eye end of a second needle to pull the ribbon over and create a slightly rounded petal edge (see Tips 6 and 7, page 48). Work petals 2, 3 and 4 and fasten off behind the petal just worked. Work remaining florets using either one or more tones, as in the photograph.

3 To make the flower centre, pull four strands of toning embroidery thread individually to create a more vibrant knot, thread into a size 24 needle and work a 1-loop French knot in the centre of each floret. Work more florets to complete.

4 To make the centre buds, thread four strands of embroidery thread into a size 18 needle and knot one end. Work 1-loop French knots at random, making sure you do not pull them too tight, mixing the colours as shown in the photograph.

5 Leave spaces between some buds and florets in which to work a few straight stitches with embroidery thread for the stems. Couch over these stitches to curve them slightly.

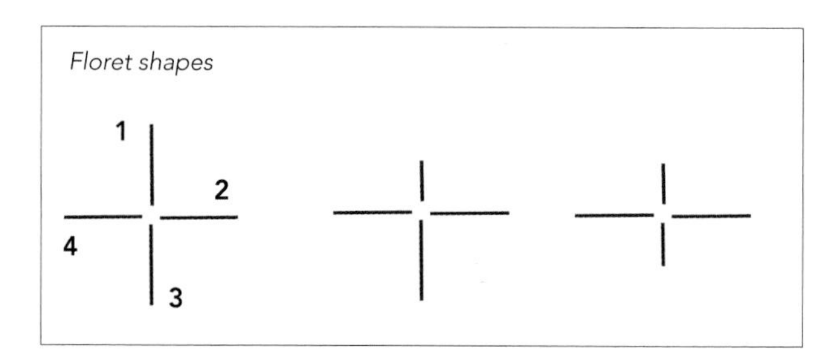

Clematis

Materials:

Approx. 25cm (10in) of 7mm ribbon for each flower (7mm ribbon is also used to make the climbing clematis, opposite)

Embroidery threads: colour for petal veins, pale and mid-yellow, plus fabric colour

Needles:

2 x size 18 needles, 1 x size 24 needle and 1 x size 8 embroidery needle

Instructions:

1 Mark the position of the petals on to the fabric as shown in the template below. Thread a length of 7mm ribbon into a size 18 needle, take it through the fabric at the base of the first petal and secure with a few small stitches, using fabric-coloured thread, behind the petal about to be worked. Now work a ribbon stitch. Slide this needle under the ribbon to smooth and place it, then take it down through the centre of the ribbon at the tip. Stop pulling immediately a shallow point is formed.

2 Repeat this, working the remaining ribbon stitch petals round in order. Now use 3–5 strands of embroidery thread to work a short, straight stitch from the base halfway along the centre of each petal using the photographs for guidance.

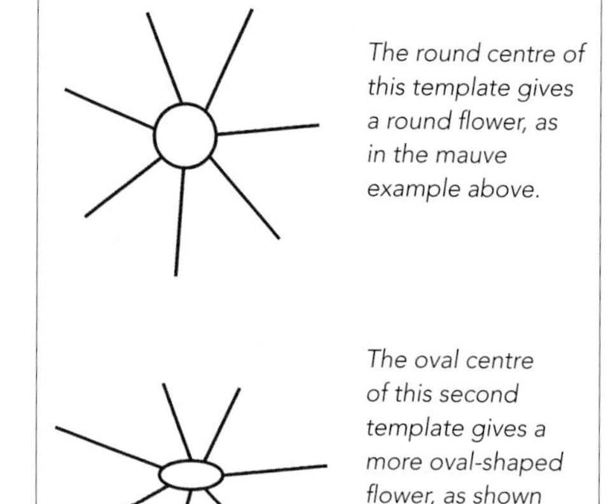

The round centre of this template gives a round flower, as in the mauve example above.

The oval centre of this second template gives a more oval-shaped flower, as shown in the climbing clematis opposite.

3 To make the flower centre, thread three strands each of both yellow threads into a size 24 needle and knot one end. Bring the needle up through the centre of the flower and back down close by, using the eye of a second needle to pull the thread over and make a loop slightly less than 0.5cm (¼in). Taking care not to pull the thread and lose the loops, work more loops to fill the centre. Fasten off securely at the back of the fabric, then cut each loop with a small pair of scissors to create fluffy stamens.

4 For the Climbing clematis (opposite), cut a length of garden string, untwist it slightly to loosen it, then couch in place with a toning thread for the clematis to twine round. Thread six strands of mid-brown thread into a needle and knot one end. Bring it up at the base of the stem and twist it loosely round the string (as in the photograph) and down the desired distance away, then couch in place with a single strand of thread. Mark the position of flowers, buds and leaves, as in the photograph. Using 7mm ribbon, work the flower petals and leaves in ribbon stitch, and the buds in straight stitch. Using two strands of thread for the flower stems, and one strand for the tendrils, couch stitch each in position with a single strand of thread to complete.

To make the climbing clematis on this page, follow the instructions in step 4.

Rose Sampler

Materials:

The samples (opposite) are worked in 4mm, 7mm and 13mm widths of ribbon

Embroidery thread in yellow, gold, green and fabric colour

Needles:

2 x size 18 needles, 1 x size 13 needle, 1 x size 24 needle and 1 x size 8 embroidery needle

Note: This rose sampler shows how the size of a flower is altered by using different widths of ribbon. The samples are worked in 4mm, 7mm and 13mm widths. Two basic stitches, straight stitch and French knots are used here to illustrate a wide range of roses and half-roses.

Instructions:

1 Using the templates (below), mark each of the petals with a dot. Anchor the end of a length of ribbon at A (petal 1) and work a straight stitch at the tip, using the eye end of a second needle to pull the ribbon over, shape and give lift to the petal (see Tips 6 and 7, page 48). Then work petals 2–5 round in order. Using two strands of yellow thread, work 1-loop French knots to fill the centre, then use two gold threads to work an outer ring of French knots with some on the base of the petals, as in the photograph above.

2 To make the calyx for the half-roses and the large bud, work three small straight stitches using 4mm ribbon for the largest, 2mm ribbon for the next size down and two strands of green thread for the smallest half-rose.

3 The left bud spray is worked with 4mm ribbon, the right with 7mm ribbon, and 13mm ribbon for a single bud using straight stitch.

4 To make stems for the buds (see the fly stitch diagram below), thread two strands of embroidery thread into a needle and bring the needle up at A, down at B, up at C, down at D and leave a loop. Then come up at B over loop CD and down again at B. Then come up at E, under AB and down at F to kink the stem. Repeat for GH and F, then bring the needle up at J to kink the stem and complete the left side bud as before.

5 To make the rose pillar, work the roses and leaves with 7mm ribbon. Secure a length of string, as in the photograph, for the pillar. Fold a length of green thread in half, secure at the base with a thread, then twist both threads up the pillar to make the stem and secure at the top. The two large roses of each spray are 2-loop French knots. Work two more pulled a little tighter and a 1-loop French knot for the smallest rose to shape the spray. The ribbon stitch leaves are secured as each group is worked, then work two colours of 4mm 1-loop French knots in clusters along the base. Add a few straight stitches between buds using green thread for grass.

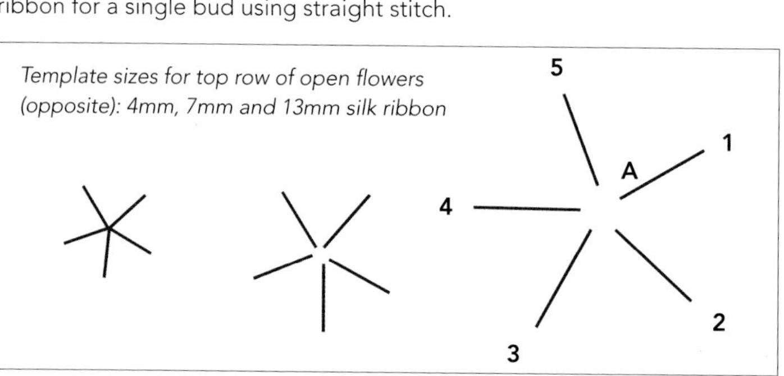

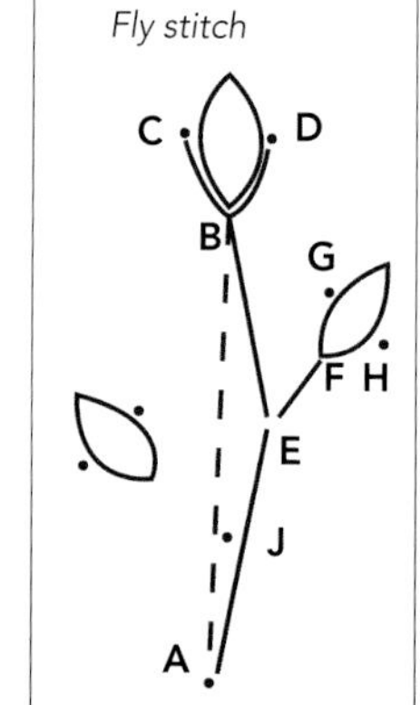

The French knots below right are made in 4mm, 7mm and 13mm silk ribbon (from left to right) and with 1 loop, 2 loops and 3 loops (from top to bottom).

Pelargonium

Materials:

75cms (30in) of 7mm ribbon in mid-pink

50cms (20in) of 7mm ribbon in bright pink

33cm (13in) of 4mm ribbon in bright pink

Embroidery threads in pale green and fabric colour

Needles:

2 x size 18 needles, 1 x size 24 needle and 1 x size 8 embroidery needle

Instructions:

1 Transfer the template on to the fabric. Mark the end of each petal with a dot (not lines across the tip). Mark each end of the buds and the stem at X and Y only.

2 To make the flowers, thread a length of 7mm ribbon into a size 18 needle and anchor it at A. Place the eye end of a second needle across the ribbon at B to flatten and keep it in place at B, then fold the ribbon over and, keeping it taut, take the needle down at the centre (C). Stop pulling the ribbon when the petal is formed. Remove the second needle, then work four more petals round in order. Using the photograph as a reference for petal colours, work the remaining flowers. Using two strands of green embroidery thread, work a 1-loop French knot in the centre of each flower. Fasten off and secure the thread.

3 To make the buds, thread a length of 4mm ribbon into a size 18 needle and knot one end. Bring the needle up at the stem end and down at the tip, using the eye of a second needle to pull the ribbon over and shape the bud. Fasten off, then work the remaining buds.

4 To make the stems, thread six strands of green embroidery thread into a needle and knot one end. Bring the needle up at X, down at Y and back up to secure it behind X. Using two threads, work a straight stitch to flower 1, as shown in the diagram, and couch it in place to curve it with a single strand. Repeat for each flower. Fasten off as each stem is worked. The bud stems are worked as before using one strand only.

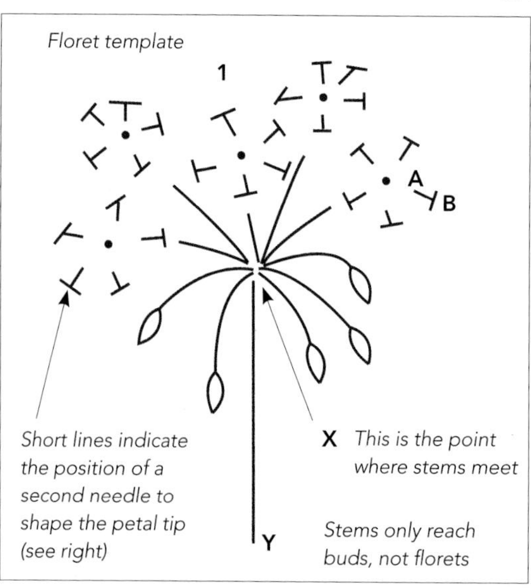

Short lines indicate the position of a second needle to shape the petal tip (see right)

This is the point where stems meet

Stems only reach buds, not florets

A second needle is placed under the ribbon to pull it over, keeping it flat and taut, as it is pulled through the fabric to shape each petal and bud.

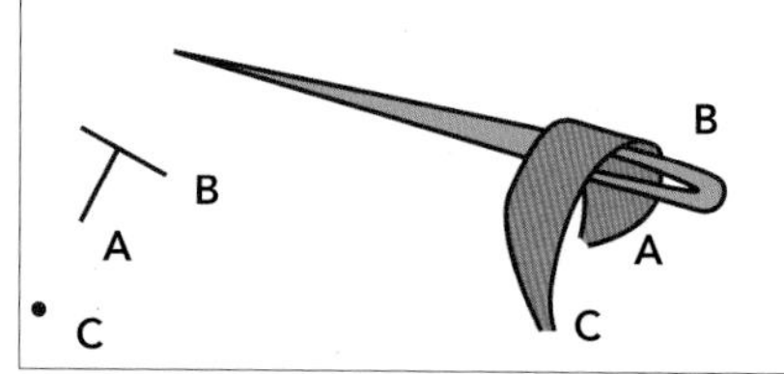

These lovely pelargoniums lend elegance and style to a plain cushion.

Thistle

Materials:

2.5m (2¾yd) of 2mm ribbon in deep mauve

1.5m (1¾yd) thick tapestry wool in grey-green

Embroidery thread to tone with wool/fabric

50cm (19¾in) of 2mm ribbon in grey/green

Needles:

2 x size 18 needles, 1 x size 24 needle and 1 x size 8 embroidery needle

Instructions:

1 Transfer the template of the thistle shape on to the fabric.

2 To make the base of the thistle, refer to diagram 1. Thread a length of wool into a size 18 needle and knot one end. Working just inside the template line, bring the needle up through the fabric at A, straight down at B, up again at C, down at D and continue across then complete the opposite side to cover the bowl shape. Fasten off. Now bring the needle up at W and down at X, then up again at Y and so on to the base to complete. Referring to diagram 2, and using two strands of grey-green embroidery thread, bring the needle up at A, down at B, up at C and down at D, 3mm (1/8in) away from AB and so on to the base, then repeat from W to X, to Y and so on to the base. Fasten off.

3 Using the same thread and a stab stitch technique (stitches that go straight up and down, not at an angle), work a tiny lazy daisy stitch over each intersection, then at intervals up each side of the bowl shape, as shown in the photograph.

4 To make the petals, work straight stitch loops with a securing knot on the wrong side (see step 2, page 12) as follows. Thread a size 24 needle with a length of mauve ribbon and knot one end. Bring the needle up in the centre at the top edge of the bowl shape and work a 1.5cm (5/8in) loop. Stop pulling, taking care not to pull the loop tight, turn the work over to the wrong side and make a secure knot (see diagram on page 12). For the next stitch, bring the needle up close to the last stitch, and continue working knotted loops to fill the centre (see Tip 4, page 48). Use a pair of small, sharp scissors to cut through each loop at an angle to create the petals.

5 To make the stem, thread a length of grey-green tapestry wool into a needle, knot one end and bring it up at the base of the flower. Cut the stem to length, use a single strand of toning thread to secure the end with a few small stitches, then work a few stitches through the stem to secure. Fasten off.

6 To make the stem prickles, thread a length of grey/green ribbon into a needle and knot one end. Work a tiny lazy daisy stitch at an angle, at intervals up the stem.

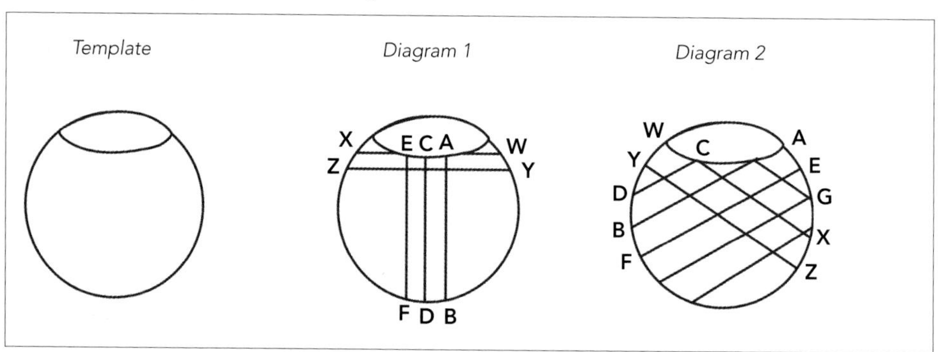

Pansy

Materials:

20cm (8in) of 13mm ribbon in the colour of your choice for the top two petals

40cm (16in) of 13mm ribbon in the colour of your choice for the four lower petals

20cm (8in) of 7mm ribbon in yellow

Embroidery thread in black and fabric colour

Needles:

2 x size 18 needles, 2 x size 13 needle, 1 x size 24 needle and 1 x size 8 embroidery needle

Instructions:

1 Transfer the template below on to the fabric, marking the points at each end of each petal.

2 Work the top two petals first. Cut the ribbon at an angle, put the point of a size 13 needle in the fabric at A of petal 1, thread with a short end of ribbon at an angle (see photographs, page 6) and pull sharply through to the back. Secure this end with a few small stitches behind the petal about to be worked. Take the needle down at B, using the eye end of a second needle to smooth and guide the ribbon over as it is pulled through to the back of the fabric, to create a rounded petal tip (see Tips 6 and 7, page 48). Secure with a few small stitches behind the petal just worked, then work petal 2.

3 Now use the second colour to work petals 3, 4, 5 and 6 in the order indicated in the diagram.

4 To make the flower centre, thread three strands of black embroidery thread into a needle and knot one end. Bring the needle up at the base of petal 3 and back down halfway along the centre of the petal, keeping it loose to preserve the curve of the petal. Work petals 4, 5 and 6 in order. Anchor a length of 7mm yellow ribbon at the centre and work a small straight stitch loop in the centre.

5 When finished, some petals may have become a little flattened. If so, reshape them with a damp cotton bud (see Tip 8, page 48).

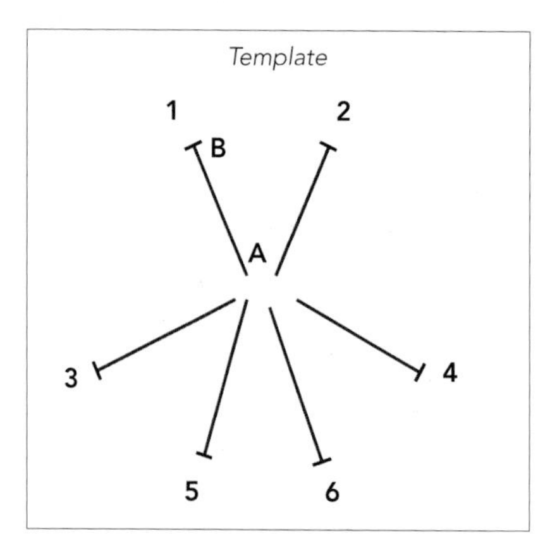

Daisy

These bright little daisies provide the perfect foil for the dark blue of a child's cardigan.

Materials:

Approx. 40cm (16in) of 4mm ribbon in white for each flower

Embroidery threads in pale yellow, gold and fabric colour

Needles:

2 x size 18 needles, 1 x size 24 needle and 1 x size 8 embroidery needle

Instructions:

1 To transfer the design, place the template on the fabric and make a dot at each end of every petal. On dark fabric, use a white or light-coloured marker.

2 To make the flower centre, thread three strands of yellow and one of gold thread into a size 24 needle and knot it at one end. Bring the needle up through the centre and work a series of 1-loop French knots to fill the centre. Fasten off.

3 To make the petals, thread a length of 4mm ribbon into a size 18 needle and knot one end. Bring the needle up through the fabric at the edge of the French knots at the base of petal A, and take it down at the tip, using the eye end of a second needle to pull the ribbon over and create a slightly rounded petal. Bring the needle up at the base of B and continue to work round in order to complete all ten petals. Fasten off.

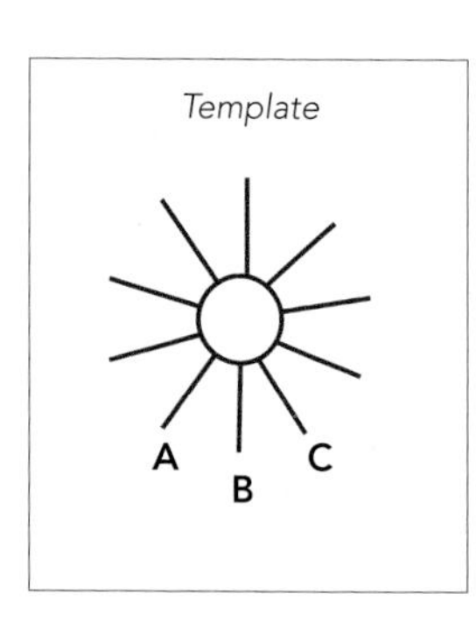

Buttercup

Materials:

Approx. 40cm (16in) of 7mm ribbon in yellow for each flower

Embroidery threads in yellow and fabric colour

Needles:

2 x size 18 needles, 1 x size 24 needle and 1 x size 8 embroidery needle

Instructions:

1 To transfer the design, place the template on the fabric and mark the dots as shown, then lightly draw in lines AB, CD and so on. (Do not draw in the outer circle; this is just to indicate the petal length.)

2 The petals are worked as straight stitch loops. Thread a short end of 7mm yellow ribbon into a size 18 needle, take it through at A and secure it with a few small stitches behind the petal to be worked.

3 Now take the needle down at B, using the eye end of a second needle to pull the ribbon over and keep it smooth and taut as it is pulled through to the back (see the diagram below). Stop pulling when a 0.75cm (5/8in) looped petal is formed. Bring the needle up through the fabric at C and continue round (see Tip 2 on page 48) to work five more petals. Fasten off.

4 To make the flower centre, thread two strands of yellow embroidery thread into a size 24 needle and knot one end. Work a 1-loop French knot in the centre of the ribbon at the base of each petal, then work more 1-loop French knots to fill the centre of the flower.

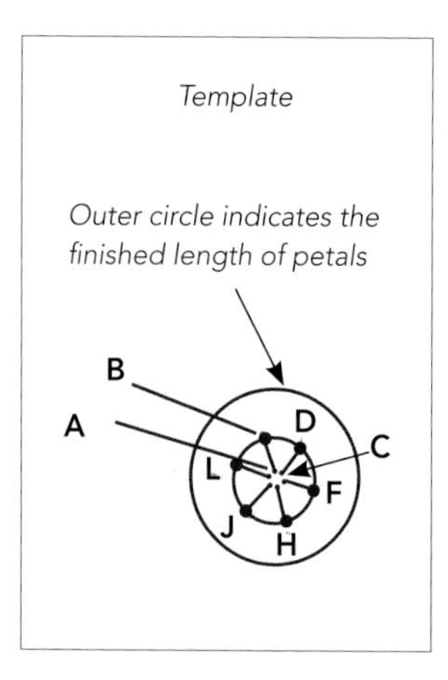

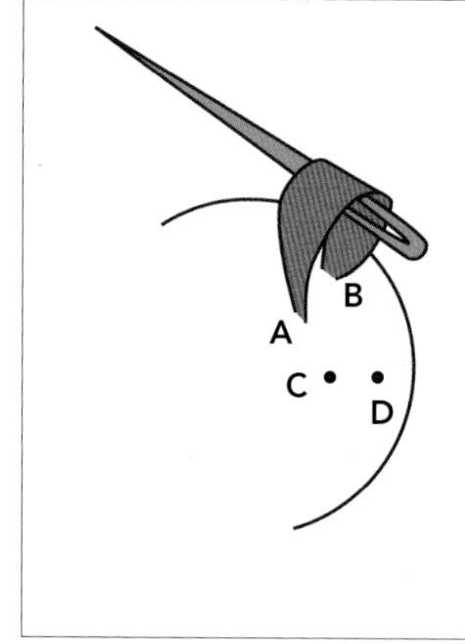

The ribbon is brought up at A, taken down at B with the eye end of a second needle in the loop to pull the ribbon firmly over until the folded edge is in line with the outer circle. It is this that gives the lift to the outer edge of the petal.

This white summer hat is embellished beautifully by the golden yellow of these dainty buttercups.

Sunflower

Materials:

2m (2¼yd) each of 4mm ribbon in yellow and gold

Embroidery thread in gold and mid-brown

Needles:

2 x size 18 needles, 1 x size 24 needle and 1 x size 8 embroidery needle

Instructions:

1 Draw a circle with a diameter of 1.75cm (¾in) (see template below) on a piece of paper and transfer it on to the fabric for the flower centre.

2 To make the flower centre, thread two strands each of gold and mid-brown embroidery thread into a size 24 needle and knot one end. Bring the needle up in the middle of the circle and work a triangle of 2-loop French knots. Then work rounds close to the first round and finish with a final round of 1-loop French knots to complete the flower centre. Fasten off.

3 Thread a length of gold ribbon into a size 18 needle, knot one end and bring the needle up at the edge of the flower centre. Now take the needle down 2mm (1/16in) away from where it came up, radiating out from the centre (see page 10), using the eye end of a second needle to pull the ribbon over to make a 2cm (¾in) loop for the first petal (see Tip 6, page 48). Stop pulling and bring the needle up, taking care not to pull the ribbon and shorten the loop. Continue working petals round in order, leaving small gaps of 2–3mm (1/16–1/8in) at intervals, then fasten off. (See Tip 4 on page 48 to avoid stitching through the ribbon at the back of your work.)

4 Use the yellow ribbon to work a second round of loops, filling the gaps left between the gold loops; make sure you always radiate outwards from the centre as you work round. Fasten off.

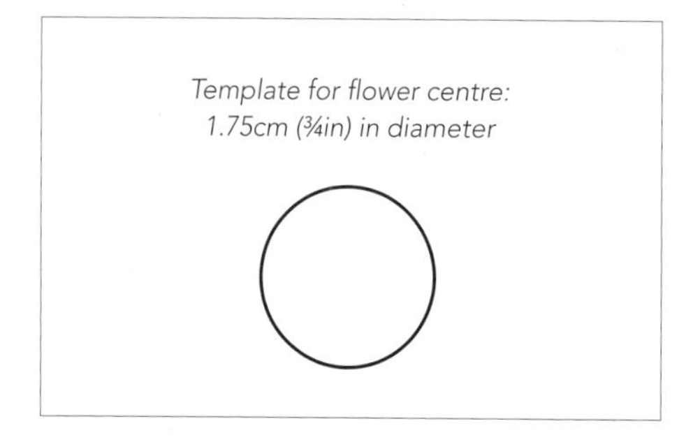

Template for flower centre: 1.75cm (¾in) in diameter

This sunflower with its looped petals looks lovely pinned to a scarf, as shown here.

Yellow Rose

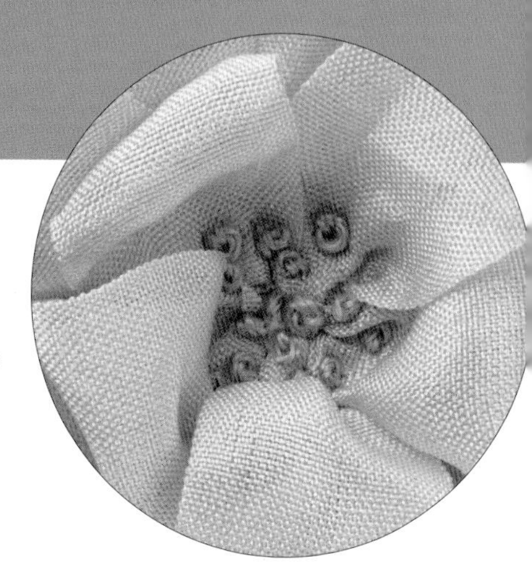

Materials:

1.75m (69in) of 13mm ribbon in yellow

75cm (30in) of 13mm ribbon in pale yellow

Embroidery thread in gold, yellow and fabric colour

Needles:

2 x size 13 needles, 1 x size 24 needle and 1 x size 8 embroidery needle

Note: For this project, shaping, controlling and placing the petals are all critical in making the flowers successfully. Please take time to read through the Know-how and techniques on pages 6–7 and the Tips on page 48 before you begin.

Instructions:

1 Transfer the design onto the fabric by drawing a 5mm (3/16in) circle on the fabric and mark five evenly spaced dots round, as shown in the diagram below.

2 Cut a 30cm (12in) length of yellow ribbon at an angle, thread a short end into a large size 13 needle and take it down through the fabric at A, securing with a few small stitches in matching thread behind the petal about to be worked (see diagram below). Now take the needle down 5mm (¼in) away and radiating outwards, using the eye end of a second large needle to keep the ribbon taut and smooth as it is pulled through, until a 1.5cm (5/8in) loop is formed. Do not cut the ribbon, but untwist it at the back if necessary, then bring it up through the next dot for petal B. (See Tip 4 on page 48 to avoid stitching through the ribbon at the back of your work.)

Template for flower centre

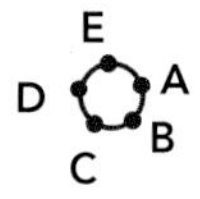

The ring of dots indicates where the needle is taken down through the fabric. Two further rings of dots will be marked on the fabric once the first and second rings of petals have been worked.

3 Work four more petals in order, then fasten off behind the petals just worked, and cut the ribbon at an angle to complete the first round. Always work an uneven number for the centre, as four petals would create a square flower.

4 Using the same ribbon, secure an end between two petals where the ribbon goes down, and work a petal between each petal from the first round, as before. Fasten off.

5 Mark ten evenly spaced dots 5mm (¼in) away from the previous round. Now work ten petals as in step 2, then a further half-round of seven petals round the lower half to give a slight tilt to the rose. Fasten off. The side with the half-row of petals will be the bottom of the rose.

6 Now mark ten dots round the edge and use the pale yellow ribbon to work petals with slightly more space between them. Fasten off.

7 To make the stamens, thread two strands of gold and one of yellow thread into a size 24 needle and knot one end. Work a cluster of 1-loop French knots in the centre and a few on the base of each petal in the centre, using the photograph above for guidance.

For the smaller rose above, a loose 2-loop French knot is worked in 13mm ribbon for the centre.

Scabious

Materials:

1.5m (60in) each of 7mm pale blue and mid-blue ribbon

Embroidery threads in pale yellow, pale blue and fabric colour

A small piece of felt to tone with fabric or threads

Needles:

2 x size 18 needles and 1 x size 8 embroidery needle

Instructions:

1 Make templates for three circles of 1.5cm (½in), 2cm (¾in) and 2.5cm (1in) in diameter and cut them out. Pin the templates in place on the felt and cut out each circle.

2 To make the domed flower centre, place the smallest piece of felt on the fabric base first, then the middle size and the largest on top. Secure all layers of felt to the fabric with a few stitches worked across the centre. Do not pull the stitches so tight that they dent the surface. Make up a thread using three strands each of pale blue and yellow embroidery thread, thread into a size 18 needle and knot one end. Bring the needle up through the centre of the fabric and layers of felt and work a triangle of three 3-loop French knots in the centre and surround with three rounds of knots. Then continue with 2-loop French knots to almost fill the flower centre and finally work two rounds of 1-loop French knots to complete the centre. Fasten off.

3 To make the petals, thread a short end of 7mm pale blue ribbon into a size 18 needle, take it through to the back of the fabric at the edge of the French knots and secure it with a few small stitches behind the centre. Take the needle back down through the fabric 1–2mm (1/16in) away, radiating outwards (see the diagram showing Ribbon control on page 10). Stop pulling when a 1.5cm (5/8in) loop is formed to create the first petal.

4 Continue working round, always radiating outwards, but occasionally leaving a 3–4mm (scant ¼in) gap (see Tips 3 and 6, page 48). Complete the round using the same colour, and fasten off.

5 Now use the mid-blue silk ribbon, taking care not to stitch through any ribbon on the wrong side (see Tip 4, page 48). Continue to work petals round in order, filling in any gaps as they are reached. Fasten off to complete.

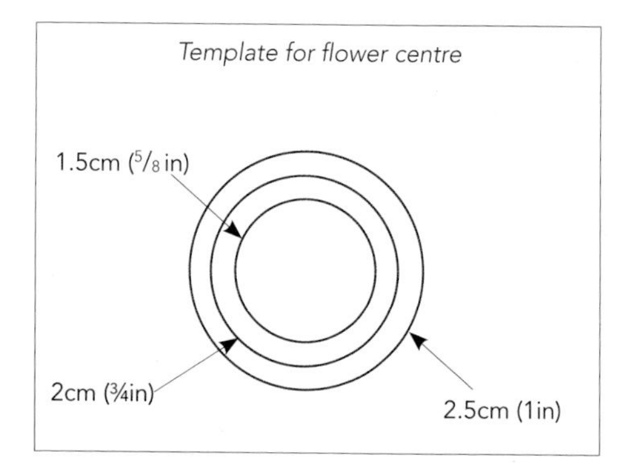

This flower has a domed centre but would work just as well without the felt padding. Pinned to a gift bag, it makes a great decoration.

Poppy

Materials:

40cm (16in) of 13mm ribbon in poppy red

Small piece of black felt

Embroidery threads in red and fabric colour

Needles:

1 x size 13 needle and 1 x size 8 embroidery needle

Instructions:

1 Do not cut the ribbon to length before it is gathered. Thread a single strand of red embroidery thread into a fine needle and knot one end. Cut the end of the 13mm red ribbon at a 45° angle. Referring to the diagram below, bring the needle up on the selvedge edge, securing the knot over the selvedge and work tiny running stitches for 6cm (2³/₈in) as shown, then back across the ribbon at a 45° angle (see diagram below). Do not cut the thread. Cut the ribbon at the same angle 1cm (½in) from the stitch line. Gather another 6cm (2³/₈in) length and two 8cm (3¹/₈in) lengths.

2 To start the flower, cut a 1.5cm (½in) circle of black felt (as shown on the template opposite), and secure it to the fabric with a few tacking stitches in the centre. Then mark positions A, B, C and D on the background fabric, as shown in the template opposite.

3 Place a size 13 needle into the fabric at A and thread the knot end of the 6cm (2³/₈in) length of ribbon into the eye of the needle. Position it so the eye is parallel to the diagonal stitch line and the cut end (see below). Hold the long end of the ribbon flat on the fabric and sharply pull the short end through to the back so that the angled row of stitches sit in the thickness of the fabric to create added flare to the petal. Using a fabric-toned thread, secure this end with a few small stitches, behind where the petal is to be worked. Take the other end of the ribbon through at B and secure this end as before. Gently pull the gathering thread to gather the ribbon to fit the curved line AB, and this thread to secure along this edge round the edge of the felt. Fasten off securely.

4 Now attach the other 6cm (2³/₈in) length for petal CD, then attach the outer petals EF and GH 5mm (¼in) away from the inner petals.

5 To finish the flower centre, use a fine needle and a strand of black thread to secure the edge of the felt with stab stitches (stitches that go straight up and down, not at an angle). This will pull it down so that it sits inside the petals.

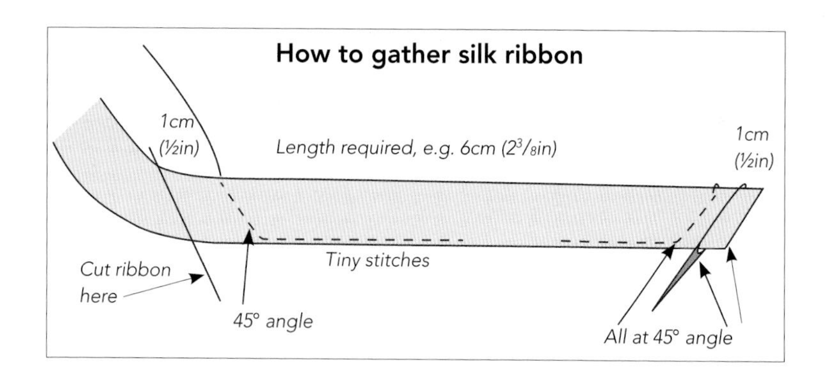

Template

C B
H G
E F
D A
Felt centre

Dahlia

Materials:

4m (4½yd) of 4mm ribbon in cyclamen

Embroidery thread in moss green, gold and fabric colour

Needles:

2 x size 18 needles and 1 x size 8 embroidery needle

Instructions:

1 Draw a circle with a diameter of 1.2cm (½in) on to the fabric as your template.

2 To make the flower centre, thread three strands each of moss green and gold embroidery thread into a size 18 needle and knot one end. Work a 1-loop French knot in the centre, then surround it with 1-loop French knots to fill the flower centre.

3 To make the petals, thread a length of ribbon into a size 18 needle, knot one end, then bring the needle up through the fabric at the edge of the French knots. Now take the needle back down, next to where it came up, using the eye end of a second needle to pull the ribbon over to keep it smooth and taut as it is pulled through (see the diagram on page 10 and Tip 7 on page 48). Stop pulling when a 1.5cm (⅝in) loop is formed; then, keeping the ribbon tensioned over the second needle so as not to lose the loop, bring the needle up ready for the next loop (see Tips 3 and 4, page 48).

4 Complete this round, then work two more rounds. To complete the dahlia, work another half row round the lower half to give a slight tilt to the flower.

The deep cyclamen of the dahlia looks very striking against dark blue and adds verve to this denim jacket.

Template for flower centre: 1.2cm (½in) in diameter

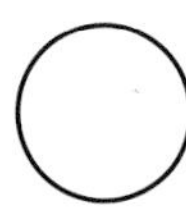

Poinsettia

Materials:

Small amount of black fabric (or colour of your choice)

1.5m (60in) of 13mm ribbon in red

Embroidery thread in yellow, gold and base fabric colour (black)

Needles:

2 x size 13 needles, 1 x 24 needle and 1 x size 8 embroidery needle

Instructions:

1 First, transfer the design to your fabric base. If you are using black fabric, use a white pencil to transfer the design. Pin the template on to the fabric and mark the position of the petals. If you are using black fabric, it is helpful if a red thread is used to work a ring of small stitches to mark the centre circle on the fabric.

2 Cut a 30cm (12in) length of red ribbon at an angle, thread a short end into a size 13 needle and take it through to the back of the fabric at X of petal 1 (see Cutting and anchoring ribbon, page 6). Secure the ribbon end with a few small stitches behind the petal about to be worked. Now lay the ribbon in position and take the needle down through the centre of the ribbon at Y, place the eye end of a second large needle in the loop and continue pulling the ribbon round the needle. Stop pulling when all the ribbon is pulled through, remove the needle and very gently pull the ribbon to form a tip to the petal, then stop pulling the ribbon again. Now secure the ribbon with a few small stitches behind the petal just worked and cut the ribbon at an angle.

3 Continue to work alternate petals 2, 3, 4, 5, 6 and 7, fastening off after each one (see Tip 4, page 48). Now work petal A as before, but a little shorter and very slightly raised, remembering to finish off after each petal is worked. Work the remaining petals, B to G, in order.

4 To make the flower centre, thread six strands of yellow embroidery thread into a size 18 needle and knot one end (see Tip 5, page 48). Work 2-loop French knots to fill the centre. Using gold thread, add a few 2-loop French knots at random to complete, then fasten off.

Template

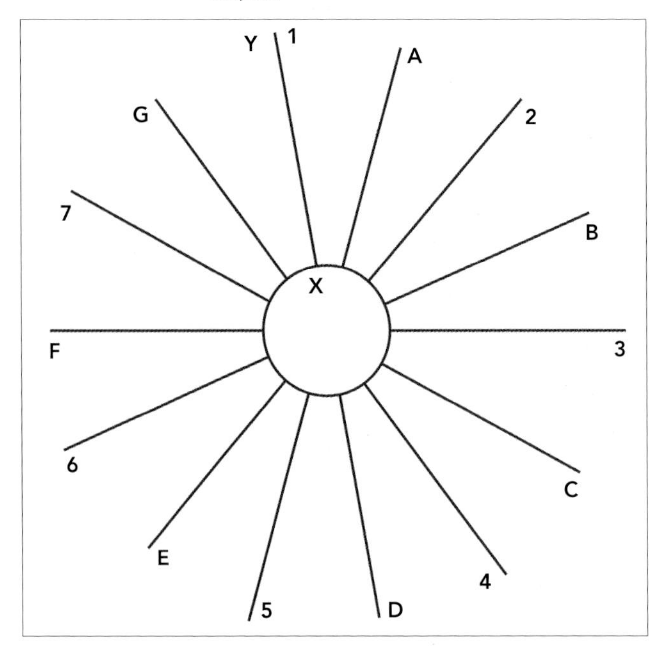

TIPS

1. **Always cut ribbon at an angle** and work with short lengths – about 30cm (12in) is ideal – as the ribbon deteriorates slightly each time it is pulled through the fabric.
2. **Work petals in order** or as indicated on the template. Never take ribbon at the back of the work across a flower centre. Stitches taken through ribbon on the back will destroy stitches on the right side.
3. **To vary petal loops**, alternate taking the needle back down either next to or directly above where it comes up each time; petals will sit differently and create movement.
4. **To avoid stitching through ribbon** at the back, drag the point of the needle across the back of the fabric to find a clear space – working petals close to each other and in order will help to eliminate this.
5. **To make up a multicoloured embroidery thread**, first separate some strands from the thread. Hold one end of each coloured thread firmly together, then select one strand of each colour and pull them out together.
6. **To smooth twisted ribbon** as it is stitched, smooth the ribbon from the fabric over the eye end of a second needle, keeping it taut and smooth on the needle as the ribbon is pulled through to the back of the fabric. The twists will disappear.
7. **To shape petals**, place the eye end of a second needle at an angle (as indicated on the template), either under the ribbon or in the loop formed on the surface, then keep this needle in place, keeping the ribbon taut over the needle as it is pulled through to the back. Only remove this needle once the stitch is formed.
8. **If petals become slightly flattened**, use a damp (not wet) cotton bud to stroke under the petal from the centre to the tip and reshape, then leave to dry naturally.